THE
ANSWER

A Handbook to Teach You
HOW to Have it All

Hilary K. Loewenstein

BALBOA.
PRESS

A DIVISION OF HAY HOUSE

Balboa Press books may be ordered through booksellers or by contacting:

Balboa Press
A Division of Hay House
1663 Liberty Drive
Bloomington, IN 47403
www.balboapress.com
1 (877) 407-4847

Printed in the United States of America.

ISBN: 978-1-5043-2677-3 (sc)
ISBN: 978-1-5043-2685-8 (e)

Balboa Press rev. date: 2/19/2015

To my husband, Kevin, and our children, Jade and Logan—
Thank you for your wicked sense of humor and fierce love.

Dedicated to my spiritual teacher, Avery Kanfer,
who helped awaken me.

To learn more about Hilary Loewenstein as a spiritual teacher and life coach, check out her website: Hilarysmindfulliving.com

Or email her at Hilaryloew@gmail.com

PRAISE FOR HILARY'S TEACHINGS

"Hilary has taught me so much about life and [about] learning to accept myself and others. Most importantly, she has taught me that having an affirmation no matter what I am going through is key. I have had to go through some tough situations during my time seeing her. I always know I can hang onto and go back to a special mantra that she and I created together to get me through. Putting the words 'I AM' in front of a sentence is so powerful. I thank Hilary for always helping me to seeing the "light" and accept that things are "exactly as they should be."—Marcie

"I have participated in Mindful Living Spiritual Group sessions for the past five years. This has opened me to meditation, chanting, and various techniques focusing on manifestation in life. Since starting the group meetings, I have come to realize and pursue a path in becoming a certified healing touch practitioner, a form of energy healing. Now that I am in the middle of this program, I have become more confident daily that I am pursuing my true path. I always knew there was something else in store for my work but just had no idea what that something was. Had I not been in this group and explored the various topics and techniques presented, I would not have had the insight nor the courage to seek this new path. I am forever grateful to Hilary."—Alice

"I don't even know where to begin. I have used many of Hilary's Mindful Living Strategies over the past several years, and they have changed my life forever. I remember she once said to me, 'Once you think this way, you will never be able to go back to the way you once thought,' and she was right. Since Hilary introduced me to the spiritual concepts and beliefs, I have never looked back. I use them every day and continue to broaden the way I think about my life, my life's purpose, and the way we are all interconnected. I can't give just one example of how Hilary has changed my life— there are just too many to explain. She is my spiritual teacher, mentor, and true friend. I thank her for all she has shared with me, and I will continue to pay it forward[s] and pass it on in my everyday life."—Amy

"Hilary's classes have helped me really start living life more fulfilled and in the moment. She teaches you how to discover your inner voice. She has opened my eyes wider spiritually. I can see and understand so much about life, how to receive and give, how to achieve and relax, and so much more. The bonding with her and the women in our group has been extraordinary. When I started with Hilary, I was dealing with a toxic friendship that was emotionally zapping my energy, I was able to let go and heal. A friend asked what my resolutions for the New Year are, and I told her about the classes and how I did not feel like I needed to make a resolution because I am attentive to living my life and giving every day. I cannot say enough about all Hilary has given to me."—Jody

"I am so happy with the way I have learned how to listen to my inner voice and live my life with passion as I focus on my purpose. I find that I am more positive, compassionate, centered, and fulfilled. I have more to give the people that I love and cherish, and I am doing a better job of taking care of myself. If you are ready, please consider joining Hilary's new Mindful Living group. You will begin a wonderful, life-changing journey, and this will be your best year ever!" —Heather

"I have always felt some type of connection to the spiritual world. Many events have happened in my lifetime [that] I was unable to understand. The strategies I learned in Hilary's Mindful Living sessions helped me to understand these events and how to apply them to everyday life. I am at peace now with several events, and I continue to use many of Hilary's strategies to resolve other issues in my life." —Beverly

"After I completed my first workshop with Hilary, I felt empowered to be me. It was much more than positive vs. negative. It was the impact of that energy on everyone else. By practicing being me, I'm responsible for me and not [for] what I think others might be thinking of me. I've also learned to trust my intuition, and that's been important for my development. Hilary's teachings have helped me evolve into a happier person and the Universe keeps opening in unexpected ways."—Debbie

"Hilary led me through each of the steps of her program with patience, real-world advice, and best of all, honesty. First, with meditation and learning to be quiet, I kept hearing that inner voice urging me to teach. But how could I teach? I didn't have a teaching degree or money. It would mean having to go back to school. It would mean leaving my kids in the care of someone else after eleven years of being at home with them. It would mean a complete lifestyle change. But through my mantra and through Hilary's support, I realized that my life purpose was to teach and be with children, for I realized that I was happiest and most content around children. Hilary also encouraged me in my faith and encouraged me to pray and rely on my faith and my angels around me. So I started to see myself as a teacher. I stopped worrying about the how—how was I going to pay for it, how was I going to find someone to care for the kids, how was I going to convince my husband this was the right thing, how was I going to be able to go back to school in my forties? Instead, I believed in the statement 'I am an elementary school teacher.' Today, I am a first-grade teacher at a school that I love. I won't lie—it was hard work to get here. I believe that once I found my life purpose and followed Hilary's program, God opened up all the doors for me."—Rosalee

"When presented with the opportunity to be part of Hilary's Mindful Living group I jumped in with the excitement of a kid going out for ice cream. Not only did it exceed my expectations, much to my surprise, it spilled over into my family. It made it so easy to have conversations about positive thought and gratefulness. I know these lessons will resonate in their mind the same way they do in mine." —Shira

CONTENTS

PREFACE

*Y*ou probably picked up this book and are asking yourself, "The answer—to what?"

This handbook provides solutions to all those questions that run in your head:

> Why am I unhappy?
> How come I never have enough money?
> What is the purpose of my life?
> Why can't I find lasting love?
> Why can't I lose weight?
> Why am I tired all the time?

While this book will not answer all of the above questions directly, it will teach you the steps of *how* to have all the things that are currently missing in your life.

You can spend your life complaining and asking, "Why me?" or you can *buck up* and become the master of your life.

It's time for you to move forward toward what you've always wanted. It's time for you to be proactive and take the necessary steps to propel yourself forward toward your goals. It's your time!

This handbook is for people who are tired of complaining and asking the above questions. This handbook is for people who are ready to do the work. While everything you could ever want will not fall out of the sky and onto your lap, the journey will be easy if you're ready to take action.

I know I can teach you how to manifest everything you want in your life because for the last five years I have been teaching people in my Mindful Living groups to do just that. I've seen great success in my groups. I've watched people awaken right before my eyes and create a better life for themselves. If they can do it, so can you.

All of the exercises in this handbook are taken from the curriculum of my Mindful Living groups. Because you are working by yourself, it may be more challenging to stay motivated. But I encourage you to stay the course and follow my steps. Do the exercises. I know there's a reason you picked up this book. You're searching for a better life for yourself. All of the steps you need to get there are in this book. You can do it. I know you can. There are great rewards for you if you do—your dreams will come true.

INTRODUCTION

*I*s it possible to have it all? I think so. I do. I am forty-six, and I have the five golden tickets: good health, loving relationships, financial stability, life purpose, and most importantly, happiness within myself.

That's a tall order, I know, and it didn't come to me right away. I worked hard for many years to build all of it. I continue to work hard every day to keep this positive vibration going. There are still days when I feel sad, defeated, unsure, unwell, and angry. After all, we are all human, and we all feel dark emotions. But the key is I don't stay in this negative vibration very long.

You can have it all too. Not only is it possible, it's pretty easy once you get the hang of it. You can manifest anything and everything you want in your life. I did. Follow this program so you can start living your best life!

Please keep in mind that God/the Universe doesn't know the difference between manifesting a castle or a button, so dream big! For example, if you are reading this book and are having extreme financial hardship, that's okay; you can still manifest whatever you desire. You can still manifest a great job, loving relationships, a nice house, peace within yourself—anything you want. It's all up to you and the *effort* you put into living your best life.

One more thing. For the purpose of this book, the words *God* and *Universe* are the same thing. I will be using *Universe* throughout this book, but if that feels weird for you simply substitute *God* wherever you see *Universe* written. I define God/the Universe as the creator and infinite source of energy that vibrates love.

What follows are the seven steps that provide the "how" to having it all. It is important to complete each step before you move to the next one. There is no need to rush through this handbook in order to finish. Take your time, and work each step until you feel ready to move forward.

Please read and use this handbook anytime you want to manifest new goals for yourself. No matter what you desire, the seven steps will effectively guide you there!

The Steps

Each chapter is organized by steps that provide explanations and exercises about how to get what you want. The steps are:

1. Know What You Want
2. Create a Vision Board
3. Visualize
4. Do the Work
5. Act on Hints from the Universe
6. Practice Positive Thought
7. Give It to the Universe

For your convenience, a reference page is located in the back of the book. It summarizes and outlines each step. You can review the reference page often and use it to help make your life plan.

KNOW WHAT YOU WANT

*W*hat do you want for yourself? How do you want to live your life? Do you want to find peace in your life? Do you want a new job?

A soul mate? A new house? Children? Do you want to lose weight? Do you want to travel? Where? For how long?

The first step in manifesting your goals is knowing what it is you really want and being specific about it. The more specific you are the more likely you will achieve your goal.

What If You Don't Know What You Want?

It's very possible and probable you don't have any idea what you want. Maybe you've kept yourself so busy worrying about everything else that you never took the time to stop and ponder your life's most important question:

What do I want?

As a kid, you daydreamed about what you wanted all the time. For example, I used to think to myself, *I'm going to be a famous singer. Everyone will want to go to my sold-out concerts. My voice will sound like an angel. I'll wear a sparkly dress and have an entourage. I'm going to live in a big house in California with my handsome husband and have one boy and one girl.*

As an adult, not so much. You are probably so busy "getting everything done" that you don't give yourself the time to daydream.

The thing is, if you don't feed your soul with dreams and goals, then you are probably often unhappy, anxious, depressed, and moody. This is not living your best life. If this is how you are currently living, then that's okay. Right now as you are reading this, you have taken the first step toward waking up! And it is never too late to change.

Get Quiet to Know What You Want

> **Try This:**
>
> *Give yourself twenty minutes of quiet time every day.*

In order to know what you want for yourself, you have to spend some quiet time alone every day. If you are always busy and have noise/stimulus around you at all times (people and electronics), I suspect you don't know what you really desire. My clearest thoughts come to me when I'm by myself. I get my best ideas while I'm taking a long shower, walking, or sitting alone in nature, driving, or sitting quietly in meditation.

Being quiet is the gateway to finding solutions to every problem. By being quiet, you connect with your inner wisdom and release your mind from everyday stressors, anxieties, and fears.

How Should I Spend My Quiet Time?

The most important thing is to make sure you are by yourself. There are many ways to spend your quiet time like: meditation, deep breathing, taking a slow walk in nature (without electronics), a long shower, a bath, listening to calming music, fishing, boating, hiking, and/or driving in silence.

Meditation Is Best

If you really want to hear your true self speak, daily meditation is the best. Meditation is so powerful because you are resting your intellectual mind. Did you know that your brain is working all day, thinking between 12,000 and 50,000 thoughts? It needs a rest! That is why sleep is so critical.

People are afraid to meditate. I used to be too. There's something about sitting still without any stimulation that feels unnerving. But with practice, it will get easier.

Most people think in order to meditate you have to sit with your eyes closed and not think any thoughts. Let your mind go blank. Yeah, right. That's probably not going to happen. Trying to quiet the running dialogue in your mind seems impossible!

I think this is why people don't meditate. They believe you have to sit up with your back straight in a cross-legged position with no thoughts running through your head. Rest assured you do not.

I meditate every morning, in my pajamas lying in a recliner with a blanket over me. Thoughts often run through my head during my meditation. I don't try to stop them. Instead, I try not to get attached to them. I picture them as clouds or balloons floating by. *Don't forget to call your mom for her birthday. What are you going to make for dinner tonight? Are you sure you didn't offend the woman at the grocery store?* Yep, they come through, and I hear them, but I don't respond to them so they just float away. If you can do this, you will begin to see your stress floating away with these random thoughts.

How to Meditate

There are many different ways to meditate. I won't overwhelm you with all of them; I'll just go over the most common:

- **Deep Breathing**—If you concentrate on your breath, you can't be thinking about your to-do list. There are many different kinds of breathing meditations you can do. I like to inhale for a slow count of five, hold my breath at the top, and then exhale for a slow count of five. I do it over and over again. You can practice deep breathing anywhere.

Waiting in traffic? Do some deep breathing. You will feel better rapidly. *(Be sure to keep your eyes open so you don't get into a car accident.)*

Breathing Tips

- When you inhale, expand/puff your chest out as far as it will go for five seconds.
- Hold your breath for five seconds at the top of the inhale.
- When you breathe out, make a "haaaaaa" sound like you're fogging up a mirror for five seconds.
- Your inhale, holding of breath, and exhale should each be for a count of five seconds.
- Visualize breathing in positivity and exhaling negativity.

- **Guided Meditation**—Various recorded meditations where a guide takes you on a journey. You listen to what the guide says and visualize what the guide tells you. I encourage beginners to try this because it's easy. It takes the pressure off you. You listen with headphones to a soothing voice, and before you know it, you're done. Go to iTunes and listen to samples of meditations so you can pick a voice that resonates with you. These days, there are also some great meditation apps you can download right to your cell phone.

- **Gazing Meditation**—This meditation is like staring into space. You keep your eyes open and stare at a fixed object. For example, try staring for ten minutes at the flame of a candle. (Have you ever noticed when there is a bonfire or fire in the fireplace, people get really quiet and watch the fire? They don't know it, but they're meditating!)

- **Walking Meditation**—In a walking meditation, the focus is not to get from one place to another; it's simply to be fully present where you are. Walk very slowly in silence and use all of your senses to notice what's around you. Listen to the birds chirping, the leaves from the trees rustling, the sound of your feet walking on the earth. Observe how blue the sky is or the squirrels you see scurrying around the grass. The goal is simply to be in the moment as an observer.

- **Meditate Using a Mantra**—A mantra is a positive phrase you repeat in your head over and over to get into a meditative state. For example, you can try: *Be still; I am calm, I am peace; Relax; All is well, I am fine.* It doesn't matter what the word or phrase is as long as it is positive and you repeat it over and over.

Catholics often use rosary beads (on left) to keep track of their prayer/meditation. Mala beads (on right) are an ancient Buddhist and Hindu way to keep count during mantra meditation. These are both great meditation aids that are still widely used today.

All of the meditation techniques help to distract your brain from thinking thoughts. When you focus on your breath, repeat a mantra, or listen to a guided meditation, you are resting your mind. And when you rest your mind you can finally hear your inner voice speak.

It is best to meditate first thing in the morning before you begin your day. But if that's not possible, fit it in any time of day even before bed (as long as you don't fall asleep). Set a timer for ten to twenty minutes and commit to meditate every day. It takes a month to create a habit, so stick with it no matter how hard it is.

Meditation is a learned practice, so you have to be patient with yourself. In the beginning, it will not feel natural. You will feel restless and want to quit. But don't! I promise after a month, you will begin to see the benefits. You will find that your entire self will feel better. You will feel a sense of lasting calm. Your head will be clearer, you will feel more certain about decisions you have to make, and your mood will be more even-keeled.

Benefits of Meditation

The benefits of meditation are abundant. Scientists and doctors agree more and more that meditation has positive effects on the wiring of the brain.

Here are just a few benefits:

Physical benefits include healing from

- pain;
- cancer;
- heart disease;
- angina pains;
- asthma;
- PMS;
- chronic fatigue syndrome;
- fibromyalgia;
- high blood pressure;
- cholesterol; and
- menopause.

Mental benefits include a decreasing of

- stress;
- anxiety;
- panic attacks;
- depression;
- irritability; and
- moodiness.

And better relaxation, memory, self-esteem, self-confidence, and relationships.

Spiritual benefits include

- increased feelings of gratitude;
- sense of unconditional love;
- general feelings of well-being;
- improved intuitive abilities;
- understanding your purpose;
- feelings of oneness with yourself and the Universe;
- knowing what to do when faced with decisions; and
- strong sense of inner knowing.

Your Inner Voice Knows What You Want

You have a beautiful inner voice that resides within you. It is the voice of truth. Some call this voice their "gut," some call it God, some call it their sixth sense, some say it's their angels, and some call it their higher selves. It doesn't matter how you refer to it as long as you understand the inner voice is your truth. It knows what you want and advises you how to get there. It will never lead you astray. It always advises you correctly. The only problem is that it speaks softly. So that's why you must first develop a quiet practice in order to hear it.

Your inner voice will guide you to what it is you truly want. And this is especially handy when you don't know.

How Your Inner Voice Speaks

Your inner voice speaks softly inside yourself. (That's why you have to be quiet and fully present to hear it). It gives you directives in very short phrases. My inner voice speaks anywhere from one word to five-word phrases.

Here are some of the directives I have heard from my inner voice:

"Call Tammi."
"Sign up for this class."
"Make art."
"Let it be."
"Relax."
"Exercise."
"Rest."
"Find balance."
"Play."
"Write a book."
"Eat complex carbohydrates."
"Be love."
"Walk away."
"Let go of guilt."

See how simple the words present themselves? Notice there are never any adjectives, negative statements, opinions, or ego in the inner voice. Only a few words that require you take action.

The inner voice speaks a directive to you right at the time you need it. For example, sometimes if I am nagging my husband when he has just come home from work, I will hear, "Be love." I feel the truth in that statement and immediately try to shift my attitude to be nicer to him.

Something to Think About:

We are drawn to positive directives. Have you noticed all the signs currently being sold in retail shops? They say things like: Have Faith, Laugh, Just Do It, Just BE, and Keep Calm and Carry On.

And think of all the songs that have been written with positive affirmations-- "Let it Be" and "All You Need is Love" by the Beatles, "Just Breathe" by Anna Nalick, "Live Like We're Dying" by the Script, and my favorite, Pharrell Williams's "Happy."

We enjoy buying and displaying these signs in our homes and listening to this music because the words are reminders from our inner voice to live our best life.

Statements You Will Never Hear Your Inner Voice Say

"You shouldn't have done that."
"John is being unfair."
"You gave a really good speech."
"You look really pretty."
"You are too fat."
"She is wrong."
"You're an idiot; why'd you do that?"

So don't confuse your ego self (the side of you that judges yourself and others) with your inner voice.

Your inner voice is the wisest voice there is. It has your best interests in mind at all times. Besides being quiet to hear your inner voice, you have to act immediately on what it tells you to do. Your inner voice is leading you to your highest and best self. It advises you on what you need to do at that moment. And because the words come so quietly, most people never hear it.

~~~

Okay, so to sum up, you need to **have daily quiet time by yourself** so you can **hear your inner voice speak,** and **you will then know what you want**.

Writing Your Goal

The language that you use to word your goal is extremely important. It is an action statement. You want your goal to be a sentence that shows the action happening *now*.

For example, one day while I was meditating it came to me that I should write a book in order to teach the spiritual laws to a larger audience. I wrote on an index card, "Write a book now."

I wouldn't want to say, "I will write a book." To me the word *will* is poison. *Will* says you will do this in the future. *Will* is a cop out. It allows you to tell yourself that your dreams will happen later. *Will* is an ineffective word because it doesn't hold you accountable now. There's no action in *will*. Replace the word *will* with *now*, and suddenly your butt is on the line, and you make yourself accountable.

Now is a powerful word in goal setting. It tells the Universe you are serious about making this happen today.

The Power of *I Am*

The other two most important words in creating your goal is using the words *I am* in your statement. These are present-tense words that tell the Universe your truth at this moment. They are commands to the Universe. These words are so important to me I had them tattooed on my wrist. *I am* is a reminder to me that whatever words I place after become my truth.

For example:

"I am married to a wonderful man."
"I am a great mom."
"I am healthy now."
"I am successful now."
"I am thin now."
"I am calm and peaceful now."

If you bookend your goals with "I am" in the front of the statement and "now" in the back, you are telling yourself and the Universe you mean business!

~~~

Before you move on to step two, make sure you **know what you want** and **make a list of your goals.** (This step may take several days or weeks to complete. That is fine. Take your time. There is no need to hurry through this process.)

CREATE A VISION BOARD

A vision board is a visual representation of your goals. It contains pictures and words of who you want to become, what you want to have, and where you want to live or vacation.

To help manifest your dreams and goals, it's important to create and display a vision board.

Every year my Mindful Living groups create a new vision board for themselves. We illustrate through pictures everything we want to manifest for the current year.

Where Do You Find Pictures for Your Board?

In the old days, all of my vision board pictures came from magazines. I still ask my friends to donate their old magazines in order to have a vast collection. I always have travel, financial, human wellness, fitness, and sports magazines available. In recent years though, I create my entire vision board by printing color pictures I find on the Internet. This makes the process easier because you can search key phrases like, "get organized," "be confident," "debt free," "in shape," and then click on "images" and quickly find the perfect photo.

A Vision Board Must Contain the Following

- **Large specific images depicting exactly what you want.** Each picture needs to represent one of your goals. In other words, when you look at the picture you must instantly know what it signifies. The way vision boards work is your eyes spend just a few seconds scanning the entire board several times a day. So you want your brain to immediately connect to the goal in those few seconds. This is why I encourage people to use mostly pictures and fewer words. Words require reading and reading requires more time. And more time means you probably won't do it, and then the vision board won't be effective.

- With each picture, it can be helpful to have a few short, positive, present-tense **phrases that enforce your goals.** For example, "I eat healthy foods." The phrase needs to be in the present tense, meaning you are doing this action now. Not "I will eat healthy foods," because that implies the future, and all power to manifest is located in the *now*. (See the "Write Your Goal" section for more detail on using words.)

- **White space.** Images shouldn't be too crowded. There needs to be space between each image so that when you look at your board, the brain can quickly and easily process each image. (Many people want to make a collage full of pictures layered over each other. While this is pleasant to look at, I have found it is not effective for helping to achieve your goals.)

- **Display the year and a picture of you and/or your family.** This is helpful because it reminds you to accomplish your goals during this specific year. A picture of you and/or your family personalizes the board.

Try This:

Create your own vision board on a piece of poster board. Use magazines and images on the Internet to cut and glue to the board. Follow the suggestions. Make sure to dedicate enough time to finish your vision board (at least two hours). Then hang your board in a place where you'll see it the most.

For the Vision Board to Work You Must:

- Spend time every day looking at the board and visualizing (picturing in your mind's eye) each goal happening.
- Hang your vision board in a place where you will see it often. I recommend the bathroom or your office. You want to make sure you see it at the start of the day and before you go to sleep at night.

- Create your vision board on a day when you have time to finish it. If you don't, it is likely you never will.

~~~

Before you move onto step three, make sure you've **decided what you want,** and you've **made and displayed a vision board** depicting your goals.

STEP 3

VISUALIZE!

Visualizing is the act of daydreaming or picturing yourself or your goal the way you would like it to be. For every goal, you must regularly spend time imagining it coming true. Visualizing is even more effective when you engage all of your senses while you daydream about your goal.

The key to successful visualizing is acting *as if* you have already achieved your goal.

For example, you want to own a vacation home. Every day for a few minutes picture your vacation home in great detail. What does it look like? Where is it located? Is there a front porch? Can you see the ocean? What do the waves sound like? Try to feel and smell the ocean spray. And most importantly, see yourself inside the home enjoying it.

Olympic athletes spend time visualizing their race—picturing themselves running on the track, observing their pace, picturing their stride, watching themselves passing their competitors to win the race!

Here's another example. You want to lose weight and look slimmer. What will you look like? See yourself *as if* you are already thin. What do you look like in a bathing suit? How does it feel to put on a pair of your jeans and have them easily zip up? How does it feel to be confident in your own body? Picture yourself walking on the beach with your new and improved body.

Children visualize all of the time. For example, they use their imagination to picture themselves having a shiny new bike. They can describe to you in detail what this bike looks like.

> "It's a green road bike with drop-bar handlebars. The bike is lightweight and I can pick it up with one hand. I can beat anyone that races me because my bike is super fast!"

Children keep their dreams alive, and sure enough, they get that bike! This is how you need to visualize, just the way a child would. You need to picture everything in your mind's eye, and most importantly, you need to know beyond a shadow of a doubt that your goal will happen.

One more example. My husband and I lived in our townhouse with our small children for ten years. I yearned to live in a single-family home on a quiet street with lots of space that backed up to a park. I would daydream about my dog running in my backyard without having to worry about neighbors complaining. I pictured going for jogs in the park behind my house. I visualized looking out my window and seeing trees and landscape with a view of no other houses. I daydreamed about a big screened-in porch where we would eat our meals and relax.

All of my visualizing worked. I now live at the bottom of a sleepy cul-de-sac. My home backs to an enormous park. All of my windows look out to trees. I have a beautiful screened-in porch where I spend almost all of my free time reading, entertaining friends, and lounging on the couch. I got just what I wanted and more.

All of us have the ability to manifest anything we desire!

Try This:

Sit quietly and visualize a goal you want. Let's say it's a new car. What does it look like? Who manufactures it? What color is it? See yourself driving on the road. What does the interior feel like? Try to smell the new-car smell. Use all of your senses to visualize and picture yourself in the car you want. (Don't forget to have a picture of it on your vision board.)

When you visualize consider some general questions:

- *Where are you?*
- *Who is with you?*
- *What are you doing?*
- *How do you feel?*
- *What do you smell?*
- *What do you hear?*

Possible Pitfalls:

- *Most likely, the voice in your head (your ego) will laugh at you. It will tell you that your vision is silly and will never happen. It will tell you to give up. Don't listen!*

- *You will forget to visualize daily. Don't stop! Daydream about your goals every day. It takes one month to create a habit. So make time to visualize every day. It only takes a few minutes.*

~~~

Okay, great! You **know what you want**, you have **made and hung up your vision board**, and you are **visualizing your goals** daily. Now it's time to move on to step four.

DO THE WORK

*T*his is the hardest part of manifesting what you want. Yep, you've got to do the work. Every day, in some way, you have to work toward your goals. Most of us feel scared and overwhelmed at where to begin so we don't even try. The thing is, you don't need to know *how* you will achieve your goals you simply need to do some work toward obtaining them every day.

For example, if your dream is to be a successful, published author, then you need to write every day. It doesn't matter for how long or how well; just write.

If you know you want to find a new job doing something that you love, then every day you must do some work to find this dream job. Research the Internet. Call any leads. Send out resumes. Ask to meet with people who are doing what you want to do.

If you want to lose weight, you have to do the work to lose the weight. Research and find the right eating plan for you. Put healthy foods in your house so you will be successful. Join a support group like Weight Watchers. Plan ahead to make smart eating choices when dining out.

We often give up on our goals because we are not guaranteed that the work we do will produce the desired result. We are afraid to take the risk. This is foolish because whenever we put work into something, it always leads us to the next step.

For example, picture yourself driving on a dark, empty road. You can't see way ahead of you, but you can see ten feet in front of you. And that's all you need to see. Once you drive ten feet, the next ten feet are revealed and so on until you get to your destination.

This is how goals work too. You can't see the entire path of *how* you will get to the end, but as you do the work, each part is revealed until eventually you get to the desired destination!

~~~

Congratulations! If you are moving on to step five you **know what you want**, you **created and hung your vision board**, you **visualize your goal daily**, and you are **taking steps to achieve your desired goal**.

STEP 5

ACT ON HINTS FROM THE UNIVERSE

his is my favorite section. Why? Because it's the cool, spiritual part of getting what you want. In the section "Step 1: Know What You Want," we talked about the inner voice that resides inside of you. I explained that your inner voice is always your truth. It directs you for the entire duration of your life on what you must do and how to get there. Well, not only do you have your inner voice, you also have an invisible support group that is always around you. They have been referred to as guardian angels, spirit guides, your guidance, and God. It doesn't matter what you call them. Just know they are assigned to you for your entire life to help you get on and stay on your life path. (I call them my angels. That is how I will refer to them throughout this book.)

What's a Life Path?

Every human being has specific talents and gifts they are supposed to share with the world. Your life path is whatever you are naturally drawn to and naturally good at. It is wherever your interest and natural talent lies. Every human being was designed to fulfill his or her purpose. Sadly, most are not. Many people feel they must have a job that pays the bills to take care of themselves and their family. They don't think it's possible to work at a job that is fulfilling *and* makes enough money. It is possible, though. And if you talk to people who have jobs that fulfill their lives' purposes and that are financially successful, they are among the happiest people around.

If you're not living your purpose, which many are not, never fear; your angels will always try to guide you back to your path.

Let's say you don't know what your purpose is. Think back to when you were a child. What did you like to do? What did you like to do where the time just flew by? Did you prefer to be with animals or people? Did you like to do creative activities or problem solving?

Now ask yourself, "What would you want to do if money wasn't an issue?" "What are you naturally good at?" Your purpose/life path resides here.

If you work at a job you hate, are in a relationship you can't stand, or are often depressed, you are not living your best life. Your angels are trying to give you signs to help you back on your intended path.

Here are some examples of how they do it:

- You continually bump into a person and think to yourself, "I really like him; I should get to know him."
- You see the same numbers over and over again. For example every time you look at the clock you see 11:11 or 3:33.[1]

---

[1] Numbers have specific meanings. Learn about their meaning in numerology books.

- You keep hearing about a book that people say you should read.
- You hear a song again and again with lyrics that have special meaning to you.
- You despise your job and your organization suddenly lays you off.

You call these things coincidences, but in the metaphysical world, we call them synchronicities. These little repeated occurrences are all part of a greater unseen plan to get you back on your life path. They are gentle nudges to get you to wake up to the life you are *supposed* to be living.

Remember that you always have free will. For example, if you want to stay in an abusive relationship, you can. Your angels will never interfere with the choices you make, even if they are destructive choices. They will only whisper and show you suggestions. So even though your intuition tells you to leave that damaging relationship, you have the freedom to make your own choice.

How I Got on My Life Path

I worked for the federal government for nine years. During that time, I hated my job. I felt like I was faking my career. It felt like I wasn't doing what I was supposed to be doing and was faking my way to get by. When five o'clock came, I literally ran out of my office and into the fresh air to finally feel free. I was physically ill all the time. I felt completely uninspired by the work I was doing. The thing is, I thought this was how we were supposed to feel. I thought everyone hated his or her job and we all worked jobs we hated to make *money*. The thought never occurred to me to follow my bliss.

My angels, however, knew I was way off course from my path. They kept trying to help by dropping subtle hints:

- I "accidentally" received a new officemate who was into spirituality. Our organization had reorganized, and we were the only two people left who didn't request an office mate. Therefore, we were paired together. Though I hated my job, I loved being near her. She taught me a lot of basic spiritual concepts. My office mate introduced me to my love of spirituality and metaphysical sciences!
- I had a new boss who was mean to me. It seemed that no matter what I did, she was not going to like me. She picked on me mercilessly. I finally left this job because she was so inflexible, and I felt like I had no choice.
- Still not getting the bigger picture, I took a similar job in the private sector. Again, I hated what I was doing but was introduced to two coworkers who were also involved in the metaphysical world. Because of them, I went to my first silent retreat,

had my first tarot card reading, and walked my first labyrinth.

- I became so interested in spirituality I went to the bookstore to peruse spiritual titles and a book called *You Can Heal Your Life,* by Louise Hay literally fell off the shelf. This book changed my life. It is still my favorite spiritual book. It inspired me so much I became brave enough to quit my job and become a full-time mom.

- My husband and I took a big financial hit when I left work, as he was an entrepreneur. I had the stable government job with a good salary and health benefits. It was a big risk for me to leave because he was just establishing his new business. He was very nervous about me leaving my job. For some reason, I felt deep in my soul that everything was going to be fine. And everything easily worked out. He started making more money rapidly, and I was very happy to be home with my daughter full time. (It worked so easily because I was finally on my life path, which at the time was focusing my efforts on being a mother).

- I kept running into people who told me there was a spiritual teacher named Avery Kanfer (helpfromavery.com) that I should go see. By the time I heard about Avery from five different people, I knew it was a sign that I needed to see him. I did and it was magic. He became my teacher for the next eleven years.

- It seemed like everyone I knew would seek my counsel. When people talked to me about their problems, I could feel sage solutions come to me, and I would help them. I kept hearing a voice from within me say, "You should get paid to do this. You are natural at counseling."
- I got a degree from The University of Metaphysical Sciences (umsonline.org). I got straight As because the classes were interesting and easy for me since I enjoyed them so much.
- I attended a spiritual workshop through the Americana Leadership College (alcworld.com). The teachers flagged me as someone who should teach spiritual principles for them.
- I taught ALC's materials for a year to a group of eight women. The workshops went so well I decided to keep teaching spiritual principles through my own curriculum that I wrote and developed.
- Five years later, I've led many spiritual groups and have a private counseling practice. I've taught many workshops, held retreats, and done some public speaking, and I am now being guided to write the book that you are reading!

You see, all along I was receiving hints and guidance from my angels to do all of this. There were signs all along the way that led me to my next directive.

(Remember the analogy of driving on a dark road. We can only see ten feet of road at a time).

Now I know that my support staff of angels are always guiding me, and any subtle hint I receive I try to follow. If you are quiet you will hear them too. Sometimes my angels will recommend healthy food I should eat; sometimes they will tell me where something I misplaced is. Often a person will say, "You should call so-and-so," and I do because I know I was guided. I know that "so-and-so" has an important message that will help me on my journey!

One More Example

For the new year, I decided to commit to eating healthier. On January 1, I looked in my refrigerator to find what I was going to eat for lunch. I saw leftover macaroni and cheese and immediately thought, "I'll start eating healthy tomorrow." I took the plastic container out of the fridge, and it fell out of my hands and dumped out all over the floor! Hmmmm... were my angels trying to guide me to a better food? I think so.

That evening, we had a family dinner at my brother's house. We ate buffet style. Not paying attention, I used my salad plate for the buffet. My mother said, "Hilary, that's really good. By using a smaller plate, you'll eat less. I'm going to do that too." And I laughed to myself, because once again, I was receiving help from my angels to achieve my goal.

You need to pay attention to the signs and the hints you are receiving every day in your life. They are always there. Many times you hear people say as an afterthought, "My gut told me to do that; I should have listened." Yes, you must listen and act immediately when your angels advise you.

If you do listen, your path to a better life is more direct, easier, and shorter. If you don't listen, it feels like you go in circles. Your angels always show you the most direct way. Sometimes the path will require a lot of courage like quitting a job or leaving a relationship. But I am sure it is the most direct way for you to receive peace.

The next time you feel this pang in your body where you hear yourself say, "What if I tried this?" or "Maybe I should do that," or "If only I could...," listen to it! Follow that thought all the way through. It is never wrong and will lead you to your best life. You will have to be brave and take action and that is scary, but the outcome will lead you where you are meant to be!

It took me a long time, but I now make all of my decisions based on what "I feel" not on what "I think." What I feel is always accurate. What I feel comes from my intuition/ my angels and is never wrong. What I think comes from my rational brain. It is based on logic and societal beliefs and fears.

~~~

Let's recap. At this point, you **know what you want**; you've **made and hung up your vision board**; you **visualize your goal**; you are **taking steps every day to achieve your goal**; and you are now **listening and acting on hints your angels are giving you** so it's time to move on to step six.

PRACTICE POSITIVE THOUGHT

his sounds easy. You're probably saying to yourself, "I do think positively!"

Are you sure? You may say things aloud that sound positive, but what do you say inwardly to yourself when no one is around?

These negative thoughts are the ones that destroy your dreams. According to *Psychology Today*, the average person thinks 12,000 to 50,000 thoughts a day and 80 percent of them are negative. That's a lot of negativity!

So let's say one of your goals is to lose twenty-five pounds. You start off really well. You are eating healthy foods. You begin a great exercise regime. You feel proud of all you are doing. But a week into the program, your clothes still feel tight. You get on the scale and haven't lost a single pound. This is the time that the negative thoughts creep in and sabotage all the good work you've been doing. You look at yourself in the mirror and start thinking, *I'm so fat, I'll never lose weight, I look terrible in my clothes, I can't do it.* Before you know it, those negative thoughts take over, you bust open a bag of chips, and you give up your goal of losing the twenty-five pounds.

This happens a lot when we want to accomplish a goal; the negative thoughts creep in and paralyze our ambition.

Here are some common negative thoughts that likely run in your head. Read them out loud so you can feel how powerful they are.

- I don't have enough time.
- I'm so fat.
- I don't have enough money.
- All I get are bills.

- I can't do that.
- I weigh too much.
- I'm so sick.
- I hate my job.
- I hate _____.
- I'm too old to do that.
- My marriage stinks.
- I'm so tired.
- No one loves me.
- I can't get it all done.
- Everyone lets me down.
- I'll never find love.
- How am I going to pay this bill?
- I'll never be able to stop working.
- I can't afford to go on vacation.

How do you feel when you read that? It's a bummer isn't it?

The moral of the story is negative thoughts are extremely powerful. If you want to live your best life, you have to teach yourself to keep your thoughts and words positive. Why?

Here's why:

The Law of Attraction

Everything in life is an energy—even your thoughts. People, animals, rocks, trees, tables, chairs, paper, and thoughts are all comprised of energy. And all energy has a vibration. Energy vibrates either positively or negatively.

Since all energy has a vibration, you attract into your life whatever you are thinking about. Your thoughts attract like-energy and like-vibration. So if you are feeling joyful and prosperous, you attract more of that to you. And if you are feeling down, you attract more sadness to you.

This is the law of attraction. Everything you think about and ultimately what you feel, you vibrate and attract. Therefore, you need to be careful and try to continuously vibrate positive.

It's not easy to vibrate positive. Once you start paying attention to your thoughts, you'll realize how many times throughout a day you think negatively. Don't be too hard on yourself, though, because most of us think negatively a lot of the time. The media, our parents, and our peers have conditioned us to think this way. (Not intentionally. They were taught the same way too!)

Most of us learned at a very young age that if we don't get the right grades, wear the right clothes, look the right way, have the right job, have the right partner, then we're not good enough. And unfortunately, most of the time we become adults and believe this!

How to Create Positive Thinking

You have to reteach your mind to think positively in order to manifest the things you want. Try these great exercises:

- **Create Positive Affirmation Signs** stating exactly what you want. Write your affirmations down and place them everywhere—in your bathroom, in your car, near the kitchen sink, in your purse/wallet. Type them in as reminders on your cell phone that pop up on your screen several times a day. Make your affirmations look attractive. Use markers to decorate them, and display them all over your home. These signs will remind you to stay positive even when your mind wants to go back to the negative—*I am thin, I am successful in my business, I have enough time, I am brave, I take risks, I am financially abundant.* Say these affirmations over and over again until you begin to believe them. Repeating positive affirmations is the most effective technique to change your negative thinking.

How to Write an Affirmation

The *language* that you use to word your affirmation is extremely important. An affirmation is an action statement. You want your positive affirmation to be a brief statement that shows the action happening *now*.

When you write your affirmation, it is very important to start with the words *I am*. Like I said in step one, these are the two most powerful words because they are commands to the Universe. They state how it is now at this moment. *I am* is a reminder to me that whatever words I place after them become my truth.

For example:

"I am married to a wonderful man."
"I am a great mom."
"I am healthy now."
"I am wealthy and successful now."
"I am thin now."
"I am calm and peaceful now."

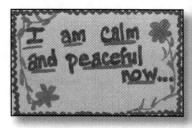

- **Reframe Negative Thoughts with Positive.** Every time a negative thought comes into your mind, train yourself to replace it with a positive. When you first start observing your thoughts you will notice how often negative thoughts pop in. Take a deep (five second count) breath in, hold, breathe out (for five counts), and say, "*Stop!* I am in control here!" And then reframe the statement with a positive.

  > "I can't do this!" becomes "I am doing this." "I look fat in my jeans" becomes "I am thin and healthy."

  It will take a lot of practice and a lot of patience to change all those negative thoughts to positive ones. Remember, it takes thirty days of repetitive action to create a habit. So don't give up!

- **Stay in the Present Moment.** This is important, so I hope you're paying attention. Did you know that negative thought comes from thinking about the past and/or worrying about the future? That's right. When you are feeling depressed, it is most often about things that happened in your past, and when you feel anxiety, you are likely stressing about what may happen in the future. It's silly when you think about it, because there's nothing you can do about what's already happened and what may or may not happen. The past can make you sad and wistful, and the future, being uncertain, makes you anxious. But if you stay in the moment, you will notice you are always okay.

> When I am upset about something, I remind myself, "That's the past; it's already happened. There's nothing I can do about it." Then I say one of my favorite affirmations, "In this moment I am fine." Once I do that, it puts me back in the present moment and gets me back on track to think positive thoughts. Remember, this is a skill you need to practice over and over again to be successful.

* **Keep a Gratitude Journal.** Before you go to bed each night, write down four things you appreciated about the day. Gratitude changes your attitude. Strengthening your gratitude will slowly create a more positive vibration that you'll carry with you all day.

> There are always things to be grateful for even when you had a terrible day. You can be grateful that your heart is beating. Grateful that you saw a beautiful hawk fly by. Grateful that a friend called to say hi. Maybe you are grateful that you have heat in your house. How about being grateful for a comfy bed to sleep

in? The more you start acknowledging all the good things that are in your life every day, the happier you will feel.

- **Find Ways to Be Lighter.** Do things you enjoy every day. Laugh, sing loudly, jump in a sprinkler, dance, play basketball, play golf, knit, make art, do a puzzle, or get together with friends. You feel better when you have fun. And having fun helps build nitric oxide, which is a wonderfully positive chemical, in your body. Increasing nitric oxide helps improve your memory, regulates blood pressure, improves sleep quality, enhances the senses, increases endurance and strength, and helps reduce inflammation. It's like the old proverb, "All work and no play makes Jack a dull boy." Don't be dull; have fun! Fun helps keep you positive.

- **Help Other People.** Whenever you help people, you create an extremely powerful and positive vibration. We are all connected to each other. When you reach out and help someone else, they benefit, and you'll notice that you feel great too!

It takes time and lots of practice to become habitually positive. Be gentle with yourself when you act in a negative/nonproductive way. Nobody can be positive all the time. Real growth comes when the increment of time you feel

Try This:

Write several positive affirmation statements on cards and post them all around your house as reminders. Use markers and make them look pleasing to your eye.

unhappy becomes shorter and shorter. And real growth comes when you can remain unfazed when someone says something negative to you.

Possible Pitfalls:

- *The voice in your head (your ego) may come in and laugh at you. It may tell you that you're not good enough and what you want will never happen. Don't listen! Instead take a breath, and say, "Stop! I am in control here!" And then reframe the statement with a positive. "I can do this!" This ego voice will get quieter the more you learn to shut it down.*

- *You may forget to practice thinking positively every day. Don't stop! Remember, it takes one month to create a habit.*

~~~

Oh my gosh, we're almost done! So, now you **know what you want**, have **created and hung a vision board**, spent time **daily visualizing your goal**, are **taking doable steps to achieve your goal, listening to whispers of direction from your angels**, and are **thinking positively.** There's only one more step left!

GIVE IT TO THE UNIVERSE

This is the last step in the manifestation process. Now that you've practiced the previous six steps, you need to let go and give it to the Universe! Can I get a hallelujah?

I know this sounds religious, but it's not meant to be. This is the final step in manifesting your goals.

After you've decided what you want; created a vision board to express it; spent time every day visualizing; done the work to move toward your goal; acted on hints from the Universe; and practiced positive thought, it is then, and only then, that you must release your grip on your goal and give it to the Universe. This means, I've done everything I can to make this goal a reality for me. Now it's time I let go and let the Universe bring the result to me.

Seriously, at this point it's out of your hands. A key word here is *trust*. Trust that the Universe will bring you the desired result. Most of the time, you are rewarded by all of your work and get what you have longed for. On a rare occasion, you don't get what you've worked for. Don't despair. If you don't, it just means that the Universe has a greater, bigger plan for you than you know at the moment. But when the time is right, it will be revealed to you, and you will understand why you had to experience what we humans call failure.

Something to Think About:

There really is no such thing as failure. Failure is your best teacher. It guides you to another option that is better suited for you.

Try This:

Right now, at this moment, close your eyes, sit quietly, and ask the Universe to help you to let go of control and trust that your dream will come true.

Possible Pitfall:

You don't believe in a power larger than yourself. You hold on too tightly and try to control everything. All I can tell you is to trust, breathe, and let go. Give it a try. If you are reading this, there must be a part of you that believes-- trust in that.

THE END... AND THE BEGINNING

*S*o that's it. Now you know *The Answer*. Now you know how you can have everything you ever wanted. Like all the best things in life, achieving your goals requires continuous concentrated effort. But you know how they say life is not a destination but a journey? That's so true. And while it is nice to achieve our goals, the sweetest moments we remember most are what it took to get there.

You can have it all. You deserve to have it all. And all the tools that you need to create your abundance reside inside you. I am only waking you up to them so you can live your best life.

I believe in you and your success. I believe that you can make the journey of your life a happy one and I hope you do too. Congratulations on your awakening!

MAKE A PLAN: YOUR REFERENCE PAGE

Step 1: Know What You Want

- Ten to twenty minutes of quiet time every day.
- The inner voice speaks quietly. You must have silence in order to hear.
- Write your goals on an index card for display
- Use words like "I am" and "now" to write your goals.

Step 2: Create a Vision Board

- Create and display your vision board depicting your goals.
- The brain needs specific, simple images in order to process them quickly.

Step 3: Visualize

- Sit quietly and picture the goal you want in detail.
- The key to visualizing is to act *as if* you have already achieved your goal.

Step 4: Do the Work

- Dedicate time daily to take steps toward your desired goal.
- If you put effort into something, it will lead you to the next step.

Step 5: Act on Hints from the Universe

- For one week, be alert for subtle hints from the Universe.
- When an idea suddenly pops into your head, act on it immediately.
- These little repeated occurrences are all part of a greater unseen plan to get you on your path.

Step 6: Practice Positive Thought

- You attract whatever you are thinking about to yourself.
- Write positive affirmation statements on index cards.
- Practice feeling grateful. It will help you stay positive.
- Engage in fun activities to keep a positive vibration.

Step 7: Give It to the Universe

- Ask the Universe to help you.
- Let go of your goal and trust that the Universe will bring you the results you want.